Wherever We Live Now

Elizabeth Rimmer

RED SQUIRREL

First printed in the UK in 2011 by
Red Squirrel Press
Briery Hill Cottage
Stannington
Morpeth
Northumberland
NE61 6ES
United Kingdom
www.redsquirrelpress.com

Reprinted 2012

Red Squirrel Press is represented by Inpress Ltd.
www.inpressbooks.co.uk

A CIP catalogue record is available from the British Library
ISBN: 978-1-906700-54-6

Printed by Martins the Printers
Sea View Works
Spittal
Berwick Upon Tweed
United Kingdom
TD15 1RS

Acknowledgements

Every writer needs four things: a good mentor who won't let you give up, a good editor who not only recognises when you've done something right, but tells you what it is, a good teacher who will show you how to create something promising out of a heap of ideas on a page, and, of course, a good publisher. So, although I can think of many other poets and friends who have helped and encouraged and supported me, I'd like to nominate Deborah Andrews, Sally Evans, Chris Powici and Sheila Wakefield for my personal awards.

Thanks to the first publishers of poems that have already appeared in print (or are in the process of so doing):

Beann n-a Sidhe, Birch Tree Englyn., the Eurydice Rising sequence, Missing, Walking on Water, and *Word to Sign: Translating Swallows* first appeared in Poetry Scotland.

A Doll for Lucy, April, Hekla's Country, Inundation, I Said, Ivy, Naming the Autumn, and *The Voice of the Carnyx* first appeared in *Northwords Now.*

Green Girl, Hjaltland, The Fall of Water and *The Green Cliffs of Moher* first appeared in *Soylesi*

Sean Nos, The Thaw and *Slate Island Landscapes* first appeared in *Brittle Star.*

The Army Camped Round Dungavel and *Visit Scotland* first appeared in *Justice and Peace*

Granary Cottage first appeared in *Gutter; Bright Morning Eilach a Naoimh* was written for the Luing calendar 2010; *Breaking Through Gravel* first appeared in *Raindogs; Goes Without Saying* was highly commended in the *Neil Gunn Writing Competition, Rushlight* was runner-up in the first *James Kirkup Memorial Poetry Competition* and appeared in the anthology.

And especial thanks to Paul, Katherine, Dominic, Naomi and Lucy for everything!

Table of Contents

Visiting the Dunbrody Famine Ship

Grief bubbles like rosin out of the pine
they built these stacked bunks from -
one to a family, and bring your own bedding,
each adult's life packed into no more
than ten cubic feet, says the ticket, including
utensils for eating and drinking.

Bad enough in fine weather, queuing to cook
in their cold half hour on deck, but in storms
battened under hatches, chewing raw oatmeal and biscuit,
sweating, vomiting, pissing in the dark,
and the smell of loss and fear. The actors recall
a good captain, five deaths only the whole trip.

It's the lists that really hurt. The database
remembers everyone, keeps them safe by name,
and age and occupation, by ship, and by landfall.
I look for my Foleys, Richard and two daughters,
my grandmother's family, left Waterford
in 1873, and lost at sea, still lost.

It's the way they tell you, as if they know
it's you, crying in the dark for your mammy,
and the sweet taste of new milk, and sunlight,
and just to be still. They know those names mend a link
in the chain that leads us back to our dead,
and makes us whole, wherever we live now.

Rushlight

Perhaps at the damp end of a dour day,
when whey-thin clouds clot and curdle
against a washed out sky, and the puny wind
sharpens the rain in my face like teeth,
I might find the rim of a blue lochan
sleeping in the cold lap of the hills, where
water-lilies fold white stars in green cups,
and reeds wade knee-deep, and whisper.

Then if the clouds would open like eyes
and, in the sudden fall of sunlight, a curlew
cry, emptying the air, and the rippled
water blink between the reed-stems -
then I would look, and listen, and grow still.
Then I would know what I came for.

Celtic Island Monastery

Beehive cells and butterflies.
Something coppery and flighty skims
over the umbels and awns of grass,
and the rare blue flowers in between,
like a glimpse of sea between rocks.

Grasshoppers whir in the soft mounds
of pink and yellow, loosestrife and vetch,
ribbed leaves of plantain, creeping stems,
saxifrage and fern. Air is full of humming bees,
and the long still space where prayer was.

Peace grew from the patient unmaking
of wrath and haste and pride. The islands' dove
brought hell with him - the guilt of blood
spilt for a book, such grief, so many souls lost.
This cell taught him the slow kindling of light.

No long-sought haven for pilgrims here.
Exiled so far he couldn't even see
the coasts of home, he would have sold
all Scotland to be back in Derry
where angels sang on every tree.

Bright Morning, Eilach a Naoimh

Atlantic sun shatters
into a thousand
diamond points of light.

Beann n-a sidhe

She hangs a line of washing out to dry,
and over lily lochans looks away
to Callanish, against the windy sky,
where tourists peer, and spend, but do not stay.

White sand and shining ocean bear the stain
of cloud, and all the western sky is dark.
The hills of Bernera are drowned in rain,
though she still hears the singing of the lark.

The crofts are let for holidays and the black
houses turned to craft-shops, tweeds and tea.
The children leave at eighteen; few come back.
There is less washing than there used to be.

It's want of heart, not money, makes us poor.
She goes inside the house, and shuts the door.

Slate Island Landscape

Stacked cliffs, and thick black slabs
provide settled horizontals,
walls, door-sills, the stepped coastline
lined and grooved, and leaved like pastry,
pocked and pointed with fools' gold.

Between the cracks, ripples foam
of thyme, black spleenwort, toadflax
and the slim prongs of grass-roots.

Verticals are finer – blunt spears
of mown flag iris leaves, reeds in flower,
hard rush bristles and sprays
of hair-grass, and seeded sweet bent,
lit with small coppers and common blues.

Wind and sea lay a blue wet-on-wet,
and on it low green islands, with cells
for pilgrims heading west, and on, and out.

Hjaltland

The Shetland Isles are green ponds
in the grey fields of Manannan.
In deep wells of time, sailors with crofts
fish for ancestors
from earth-house, ring-fort
long-barrow, castle, hermit's cell -
the place where land is sea, is home,
is grave, is memory, is life.

Mousa Broch, Jonsmass

Midnight sucks the colour
from sky, sea, rain-wet grass.
A flicker like a shadow
curdles the skim-milk twilight,
an inky wisp of dark wings
jinking, wheeling round the still
bulk of weathered ruined fort.
Sharp flight threads the gaps,
stitches the hollow hill
with six thousand nests.

The broch of stone and feathers
blind watch tower, gives breath
and blood to the slow drift of time.
It bubbles and simmers,
a stock-pot of wheezy petrel voices,
long tickings, and a shrill 'a-haaaa!'
airy and thin, as if they came
from alien wind-pipes,
voices far away, music of the ghosts.

Poems to the Sea by Cy Twombly

Twenty-four slabs of white on white
blue constant horizon   paint splashes
faint wisps of pencil

Mediterranean white white white
and when the sun comes up
becoming a lighter white

wave current ripcurl swell
weed flotsam bubbles spume
implicit goddess

painting the process of water
flows and falls of cloud
rain meeting ocean

painting the process of poem
words aimed shifted   retracted
mind meeting paper

scribbles arrows overlays
the shape it takes on the page
the reveal in the process

Goes Without Saying

The Languages of Nicaragua

1.

In the cloud forests live two old men,
the last speakers of a tongue
that remembers those who made
the footprints at Acahualinca.
They have words for every orchid,
and all the unrecorded ferns and fungi,
the moss, the crops, the weather, treefuls
of birds like flying gemstones,
the mist and smells of home.
They have had a falling out.
Now they don't speak.

2.

In Villa Libertad four hundred
deaf children fail to connect
with their teachers' Spanish.
Lip-reading and finger-spelling
cannot name their world. Instead,
in street and school-yard they combine
their family signs to greet, play, comment,
shape their day. In their fluent hands,
mimicas acquire nuance, grammar, syntax.
In the Idioma de Senas de Nicaragua
they speak for themselves.

Word to Sign: Translating Swallows

Scissors in the sun,
the flight of swallows
neatens the May garden.
Busy beaks bristling,
a loop, a touch and away,
they trim summer's petticoats
with spangled ribbons
of pollen and midges.

Katrina's poem
is soundless,
composed in movement,
the logic of sign -
a whole body conversation.
Nuance and accent show
in subtlety of gesture
mobility of face
the discipline of posture.

She shows us speed,
grace, a sudden swoop,
the ownership of air.
The pun of gulp and flight
becomes a dance, a bird,
embodied memory,
that lawn, that sunlight,
that transient summer.

I Said

Round and glowing,
curved, I said, and glowing,
sharp and sweet and bitter and hot,
and gold as guineas and sunlight,
and burning, I said, globed and burning
and piercing, pungent, all those words,
and sweet, and fresh, and dripping,
look, and taste, and smell.
All the words I said.
I meant oranges.

Missing

The sound of the wind
is your footstep on the stair.
The rain on the window
rustles your sheets.
The house is not quiet without you.
You are so noisy
when you are away.

Green Girl

Crossing that adolescent threshold
into a more than rational universe,
I found myself among herbs -
leaves of jade, glass-green, ice-grey,
and smells that open doors -
a ghost of lemon, breath of mint,
the bitter medicinal tang of yarrow,
rosemary - a scent of pine and dust
and memory - and the clean
kitchen smells of thyme and sage.

Here naming was blurred.
Hedge became garden, became flower,
became food. But knowing was clearer -
lavender was not prim at all,
but hot and heady, with a hint of camphor,
incense, resin, honey, spice.
Roses bloomed in flamenco skirts -
a fiesta of apples, myrrh and incense,
all soft, but warm and wild, all different.

In those green years I grew my roots,
learned daring and defiance, reaching
with sense and spirit into the earth,
old wisdom, the skill of hard work
in mind and muscle, the way the weather
shapes our growth, the life of birds,
new tastes, the feel of my own magic.

Ivy

It is the vigour that amazes –
the lithe sprawl over the rockery,
the spring and spurt up telegraph poles.
Stems in pin feather up as fast
as April's hatchlings, become a cloak
of pentacles, witchy jade-veined green
full of sparrow's nests, barbed with feet
like caterpillar's feet, dug right in.
Its extravagant adaptability
and hospitality to bees
make it seem domestic.
It is not. Its massed and twining weight
will bring down oaks, and institutions.

Birch Tree Englyn

Seed tree, weed tree, the shining silver birch
grows in the waste places.
Pioneer on the peat hags –
forest trees root in its wake.

Inundation

There has been a flood. The rising blue
fills the hollow space between the trees,
and washes over hillocks with a strange
still completeness, as if the sea had learned
to flow uphill. I will remember this
when pods of dolphins swim through Marble Arch,
and divers pick up rusted mobile phones
from silent oyster farms on Princes Street.
I will remember then the sunlit spring,
and Aberfoyle's green braes, drowned in bluebells.

Christmas

The alchemy of myth-
the stars and angels, the earth's
return to light, green ivy,
the quickening sap in the tree's
deep heart, the cattle
kneeling in frosty fields,
the robin's song at midnight -
all refined to the bare particular
fact of a birth -
that night, that inn, that boy.

The Last Snow

A stealth of snowfall
dizzying into the dark, drops
a boa on the boundary wall
of swans' down and diamonds.

Its weight makes white lava fields
of lawn and yard, with sink-holes
where bird breasts and cats' feet
have warmed through to the stone.

Wind sweeps and scours it
leaving slopes naked,
fills hollows and hedge-banks
with cauldrons of ice.

Frost shines and hardens it
to a ruffle of bony lace,
bleeding whiteness in the sun,
transparent, crumbling, gone.

Tentative

A dunnock crosses the March-dried herb patch,
a ruffle of shadow as if a breeze
put out a hand to caress the juniper,
and changed its mind.

A crocus unfurls a golden fan,
airily flirts with a sun-drunk bee.
Sober clouds pull themselves together.
The fan raps shut.

A drift of sunwashed drizzle.
A quilted sky, stay-stitched with northing geese.
The sullen wind flings a fist-full of rain
into the pond, moves on.

The Thaw

Just two degrees of difference.
The air softens and dulls, grass blurs.
The privet heights are quick with sparrow-bustle,
blackbird hop, wren flit, a new colony
born in craic and kerfuffle.

A great tit trapezes birch-stems
nibbling the catkin sheaths,
the see-saw strop of teacher, teacher,
sharpens the morning, adding fizz
to spring's still coolness.

Ebb-tide is swimming with ducks,
upended, spinning, suddenly noisy.
Paired swans, humped leavings of snow,
melt into the drained river.
The slick banks slump into silty furrows.

Damp is gathering with the first drift of rain.
Earth relaxes ice-bound muscles,
lets out the sharp sour stink of thaw -
mud and leaf-mould, and frost-burned grass
collapsing into wetness, rot, fertility.

Washday Morning

The wind sashays through pale sunlight.
Green thickens in the orchard
and in the gardens washing sways
on the sagging lines. A blackbird hen
stuffs moss into the scaffolding
of her nest in the bay tree.
I cut up words for poems,
watching the spring walk into Stirling
in a stealth of ash cloud and new grass.

The Fall of Dark

That fluid, illuminating moment,
which stabbed like a knife and pulled
our whole life out of shape, has melted
like snow on a ditch, leaving
a fading glimpse of swan-wings,
a handful of reeds, Molly Bawn
dead in her white apron, the echo
of bittern and rain-goose calls.
Even the memory seems trivial now,
a spook-light, not worth mourning.

The Forth is at low water.
Cormorants hang their silent wings
among the plastic bottles, cans,
cling-film and mutilated dolls.
The dark congeals, a loose drab wash
slicks huddled clouds with fumes
of diesel, alcohol and piss.
Epitaphs on subway walls record
the feral rites of teenage loss.

This cannot last. The tide has turned.
Something stealthy and profound
moves like the upward drift
of water through capillaries.
Faith, choked and demythologised,
revives in flags and wind-chimes,
clootie-trees and talk of omens.
In the late leaves of the ash tree,
the thrush drips song into the dawn.

Spring Equinox

Gulls neatly surfing a south-west wind
gritty with frost.

The flutter and drunken swing of shirts
strung out on the line.

While you were thinking of something else,
a curlew's song.

Hawthorn unwraps prickly new leaves
a scumbled haze of green.

Black and white on the muddy river-bank
oyster-catchers whistle.

The river hurries with its load of silt,
jostles the reed-beds.

A ripple of goose-wings flowing north -
cries waking the spring.

April

How pale and cold I look.
Frosted grass is soaking through shoe-leather.
The smell of hyacinths.
The oblivious busyness of birds.
You will say,
'This came out of nowhere.'
You have not noticed the small signs -
a change in the wind, the clearing skies,
a cold, biting breath on your cheek.
The gravel rumbles under my feet.
I will not look back.

The Fall of Water

written at the Little Fawn Waterfall, The Duke's Pass, Aberfoyle

The lithe leap the river makes
demands its own vocabulary
as ballet does – technical, evolved, exact -
to match its lacy, poised deliberation:
 grand jetée,
            failli,
                        sauté de chat.

Rocks heaped in the rift,
frayed and grained by its passage -
a mouthful of teeth, with splintered branches
caught between grinding edges.
Some are weathered like knuckle-bones,
others patted to a fat-buttock roundness,
one a perfect ogee, like the keel of a boat.

In the dapples of the trees a dust-brown moth
abseils down the reveal of sunlight and is lost
among bracken, the stealth of birds
and the sleepy conversation
of water slipping between stones.

Midsummer Haikus

Summer Rain

When the long drought ends,
rain kisses dusty windows,
whispers on the roof.

Grey June

Grey June twilight now.
Rocket scents the still garden -
cinnamon and dew.

Harvest Moon

Glossy rich moonlight
butters the sliced cumulus,
melts into the night.

Autumn Equinox

Blue fallen stars -
whiskered flowers of borage in the grass

brown-gold bees tumble
drunken carouse in silk poppy cups

red admiral fans
fiery platefuls of bunched autumn joy

willow warbler flit
green-gold between crimped rowan leaves

gabriel hounds hunting
grey lags calling the dead of winter.

Naming the Autumn

A mite in the hills' green folds,
I walk, naming the autumn –
coal tit, oakmoss, bracket fungus.
I mark the whiskered outgrowths
of blaeberries and whin, and hollows
where primroses will flavour spring
with sunlight and honey. I know
which woods are good for burning
and where the Highland fault line cuts
the ancient metamorphic rock
from fertile sandstones in the south.
A net of sweeping birch twigs sifts
the wind, and catches strands of lichen,
ice-green and hairy. Taxonomy
fails me. I cannot bring to mind
its name, or whether it's the sort
I need to make a winter pot-pourri.
No matter. The art of knowing
is knowing when to let things be.

Hohokam

In the street, the grey dust blowing
stirs up the bus tickets, fag-ends,
slips from the ATM, the good intentions,
the comebacks, the make-ups, flirts,
recriminations, the killer pitch.
All dropped and forgotten.
Swirled against the wall.
Left out in the rain.

Cast-offs

The Red Crag grins -
sandstone teeth in green face.

Wind and sand on the beach
flay bark off a dry branch,

grind small cupped shells
to scalpel-thin gleams of pearl.

This flint is knapped. Hands did this -
knocked the edge to a point, dropped it,

discarded, as the cliff discards
six feet of stone and grass each year.

The abandoned flat hump of lighthouse
waits to be dropped into the sea.

A Doll for Lucy - The Orkney Venus

It would have taken time without metal -
hours, weeks, grinding the stone to part
the head from the shoulders, score the lines
that gave her hair, hands below wide sleeves,
the flow of her dress and the pins
that kept it together, like owl eyes, like breasts.

Who else would they have done it for, endowing
two inches of pebble with wisdom,
her mother's fertility, her father's smile,
the memory of hills in her brow-line,
the lochs of home in her eyes,
except a loved child?
                              More than a play-thing,
they made her a doll to keep in her pocket,
a blessing of family, homeland and story
to keep her safe, as we would keep you.

Museum Exhibit at Arles

Two thousand years ago they put the child
to sleep in the cupped length of a roof-tile,
as in a cradle. Her longer bones
are fine as knitting needles, the small skull
sunk into the cavity of her crushed ribs.
Behind glass walls, earth and ash cling to her,
and the smudged caressing fingerprints
of mourners long since gone to clay.

The Army Camped at Dungavel

For the Eurydice Socialist Women's Choir, Glasgow

The Eurydice choir
sings as if at Jericho,
as if the new loud hailer
could break Dungavel's walls.
A butterfly, sun-fuelled,
rides the autumn wind like ocean,
makes land-fall, leans its burning
trivial weight against the steel.
To move a mountain, faith
needs such moments of temerity.
We do not know our strength,
the butterfly and the choir.

Border Lament

For Richard Ashrowan

grass in the wind
a trapped white feather

river flow
the sound of wind

cross currents in the water
reeds quiver

leaf on the stream
flows over stone

sunset light in the mist
red as blood in the water

in a place odd and empty
the whole world opens.

The Voice of the Carnyx

The Prom is at Glasgow green -
a field of tartan rugs, of crisps,
wine, chocolate and folding chairs.
Texts ticker-tape the wide screen –
greetings, jokes, the mandatory proposal.
Saltire and lion rampant wave,
eclipsing the lone union flag.
A golden moon climbs the sky
lost in the white blaze of arc-lamps.

The carnyx stirs like earth awaking,
boar-headed, goose-necked,
its red tongue lolls, eyes glitter.
War-cry and battle-standard in one,
it has the sound of bittern and curlew,
of rutting stag, and the deep continuo
of bog and stone and heather.
It sings in the park with Pictish voices,
with the memory of deep past,
lost grudges, ancient wrath.
Its name is Legion.

Visit Scotland

Dungavel makes a grim landlady,
corseted with steel, her flinty face
edged with fat curlers of barbed wire.
She keeps her eyes shut when we come,
plants police like knuckles at her hips,
more of them, this time, than us.
You asked so little when you came –
an ordinary life, work, shopping, school,
a joke with the neighbours, uninterrupted sleep –
Scotland could not manage even that.
I bring you shortbread, and caramel wafers
wrapped in tartan cellophane.

Hekla's Country

Hekla, 'the hooded', stands on the skyline.
She broods over a sorcerer's country,
her bitter, burning malice cloaked in snow.
She is the origin of the sulphur reek,
the cinder tracks, the clouds of dust,
the streams which run ice-blue and steaming,
and the thin soil, bound with roots of lupins
like cobalt flames among the knee-high pines.

She is the gate of hell. When she erupts,
she fills the air with ash and poison
and, for months, the sounds of souls in torment.
She buried Gaukur's house at Stong
metres deep in tephra. Yet her fields are green.
The hills above the whale-backed sea are curved
as softly as the flanks of sleeping cats.
They chalice sun and wind like wine.

Her wiles ensnared Gunnar Hamundarson.
The witch betrayed him to a hero's death
with strands of Hallgerd Longlegs' golden hair -
that's how they tell it now. The saga says
Hlidarend was too beautiful to leave.
His horse stumbled, and he looked back
at golden cornfields and the new-mown hay.
I'm going home," he said. "I will not go away."

The afternoon I stood at Hlidarend
below the church, and looked out at the sea,
I thought of Gunnar singing in his grave,
and understood. My heart roots in this place.
I long for Hekla's country in my dreams.
I keep a piece of tephra on my shelf,
and sometimes sniff my jacket seams for dust
that smells of sulphur, rock and Iceland.

The Bower

They bought it for holidays, a place
where rain fell more softly, new flowers
scented the hedgerows, and the kitchen
smelled of earth and bread and roses.

But love is always another country.
A glance, a kiss, the touch of a hand
and you're over the border before you notice,
in foreign territory, where all the laws are different.

She said, I'd like to live here always.
He tied the whole house in blue ribbons
and gave it to her. When he left,
she had nowhere else to go.

Zen Shoes

The shoes are at the door -
green ballet pumps, lined at the toes,
bright clogs of blue suede, thick-soled trainers
with grass and dried mud in their grooves.
Zen is not practised in shoes.
We sit, learning stability,
facing the wall, anchored and aware
of cracked plaster and spider webs,
pale blistered paintwork,
our minds stravaiging the stillness,
and our shoes, waiting at the door.

Walking on Water

The trick is to keep moving,
face forward, never look down.
The jelly swell beneath your feet
melts under your gaze, and small fish,
silver against the glittering sand,
flit from your sudden gravity.

The trick is not to look inwards;
Don't watch yourself doing it.
It's important to look away
to where stone houses on the cliff
draw closer, and the white waves
play chap and run on the sand's door.

The trick is to put your faith
in willing hands stretched out to you,
in those others who take for granted
the paradox and adventure
of walking unsupported
solid on the crest of the sea.

Little Sister

"A poem --- tells how much fiercer the beasts would look if they weren't restrained by respect for the sultan."

quoted from the Rough Guide to Andalucia

In the Sala de los Abencerrajes,
beneath the dripping mocárabes,
the blood of sixteen princes
stains the fountain. The rill flows
between the gardens, paved now,
to keep the stones from damp.

A cat threads the shadowed space
between the pillared feet
of ten stone lions, squat and impassive.
Their broad backs and eroded manes
are shelter from the insolent heat
and stares of strangers in her court.

She is queen here, her silken sandy coat
brocaded with lithe muscle, and soft feet
clawed with ivory scimitars.
She drinks from her pool at the feet
of her stone brothers, ferocious,
untamed by any sultan, and alive.

Pentire 11th August 1999

Before the eclipse, stalls selling tinfoil glasses.
After it, ice-cream and t-shirts,
and in between, the shifting sky, and shouting -
Go on! Go on! as if the clouds could hear us.
A man's voice behind us, thick with drink,
Cajoles it in a buttery lover's croon -
Let's all think of flowers, and good things!

A silver fire swam in a sea of cloud.
The black moon bit a chunk of sun.
Gulls screamed, dogs barked,
the sea faded, the headland wore a shroud,
maroons wailed in the vampire light,
and we waited for it to be cold.

The clouds thinned and we saw
the diamond ring, corona, Baily's beads.
Light sprayed out from behind the black circle -
the moon's lid on a jar too full.
When the sun pushed it aside,
the headland breathed in colour
breathed out cheering and souvenirs.

Everyone told a story of that day,
that summer, ten years or more ago,
and the world has grown warmer, not wiser.
In the new eclipse we hide, expecting
apocalyptic horsemen, not good things.
I have never since heard anyone
talk like a lover to the sun.

India's Alchemy

For India Flint

How she simmers mashed leaves,
shredded roots, pounded bark and berries
until the colour flows, and bleeds
into kettles, and stains her hands,

how the mordant bonds and brightens,
and how the air transforms
the white to rust and umber,
green indigo to bright blue,

and how some stains are welcome.
Silk drinks up the sap of leaf and flower,
colours different every time, and shapes
a ghostly faded permanence, like memory,
like what our hearts are steeped in.

Lir's Children

No wonder they thought of swans
in the fields and bogs of Donegal,
and the wide skies of Meath, where birds
from Iceland bring in the winter.

No wonder they thought of swans
where the chambered stone at Bru na Boinne
mirrors the starry bird, whose bright eye
guides home the wandering sun in spring.

No wonder they thought of swans
who travelled like songs and monks,
lost lovers and warriors, between the cliffs
and green coasts of Alba and Eire.

No wonder they thought of vision
'let loose like a swan on a river',
the freedom of wide white wings,
and the wisdom of sweet Irish.

I think of children exiled and caged
in the narrow coffin of a swan's breast,
transient as tinkers and tattie howkers,
their songs keeping them together.

And after it, the homecoming,
Tara's bare hearths and changed days,
the thin sound of church bells, and the last
liberation of holy water.

Sean Nos

The stillness of the old musicians,
singing at the bar's end, eyes closed,
is a thing you wouldn't notice, unless
you sing yourself. The skill doesn't show
in dynamics and drama, it's rubbed hard
down into the song's grain till the voice
glides silky and free and nothing comes
between mind and melody. Sean nos
is of the soul, a music gathered,
in-dwelling, sung from the quick of the heart.

The Green Cliffs of Moher

On the green cliffs of Moher,
the square white lighthouse shone a last farewell
to the emigrant ships a day out from Cork.
Now the wind sings the theme tune
of the great discontinuity. Third generation
Americans look through rusted telescopes
over the grey, bird-starred Atlantic
at the ghosts of ancestors looking back.
Oblivious gulls filch crusts from picnic bags.
I look for drowned Richard,
Katie and Bridget going to Colorado,
but my heart is not in it.
From the green cliffs of Moher I take three white feathers,
souvenirs not of lost Eden, but of flight.

At Corcoran's Bar, New Ross

Old men in Corcoran's Bar sat in a circle
in the long room beyond the bar,
last made over in the eighties, and gone to seed.
A session, I thought, for tourists.

It was what I'd hoped for – all familiar.
Love Is Teasing, The Rocks of Bawn,
King of the Fairies, Vinegar Hill.
Old songs in good hands fit and moved
as easy as the handle of a well-used knife.
Nothing new, no spit and polish, just right.

"Come into the engine room," they said,
invoking the myth, and I took my place
on the hard leather seats among the elders,
and sang for them As I Roved Out.

"You sang that very nicely." Kind words
that put me in my place. If I lived here,
I'd be in the back seats for years, joining in
the choruses, until I'd learned my craft.
These old musicians could have been to school
with Packy Byrne, O'Carolan, Aengus Og.

Inside, the sounds of fiddle and accordion
as we left, taking the music home.
And outside, the cry of a wild swan
coming in over the sea of Moyle.

Granary Cottage, Wexford

Here are insects still at pest level -
three-piled spiders' webs, scum-coloured
flies buzzing the fruit bowl, thin mosquito whines.
I think of bites and stings, and dirt piling up
in uncleaned corners, and remember
tacky coils of flypaper, and beaded nets
we used to cover food with, and don't need now.
Those are things I never thought to miss.

What's lost becomes exotic.
Bitterns, kites, and corn-crakes in the fields,
that sound like broken gates, and have become
desirable as skylark, thrush and nightingale,
are valued when they're gone. This cottage
where the wild and human have to co-exist
on terms I didn't set, and can't control,
is alien now, and not quite wonderful.

Ireland is my lost country.
These hollow ash-tree-shaded lanes
and lush wild gardens, where the Mermaid rose
blooms among nettle, thorn and fuchsia,
are where I wish I lived, but know I can't.
Something squalid and inconvenient,
yet vital, thrives here, that I have lost
the skill of living with, and can't get back.

Glendalough

Bury me at Glendalough,
where the water falls like a white knife
between the black rocks,
and the huddled grey tombstones sleep
at the foot of Kevin's tower.

I want to be by the lough's wide blue sheet,
where kneeling Kevin
heard blackbirds and red squirrels
sing lauds and vespers
from his lonely stony bed.

I want to hear children come
to the new centre of pale wood and glass
to learn how books were cherished,
and monks sang in praise of a God in whom
their parents say they have no faith.

I'll rest within the sound
from the bright red van selling hot dogs,
and the hawkers making money
from shamrock, and green stone rosaries
and whiskey-flavoured toffee.

Bury me at Glendalough
because my people know themselves there.
There, not at Tara, nor O'Connell Street
is where they know their origin,
and where they want to end.

Eurydice Rising

A multi-layered and open-ended sequence of poems based on the Orpheus legend as re-told in the Classical, Breton and Shetland versions

The classical story of Orpheus is simple and well-known – Orpheus' beloved wife is stolen by Hades, and dies. Orpheus goes to the underworld to rescue her and plays so well that he is allowed to take her back, so long as he does not look behind to see if she is following him. He does look back, and she is lost forever, and Orpheus, distraught, is killed by Maenads because he refuses to play for them. This story is told in many cultures and many formats, but what fascinated me as I got to know more about the tradition, was that as the story was dispersed and retold, versions developed which did not end with tragedy. As the story moved north, it happened more and more that Orpheus actually got Eurydice back.

The many symbolic values encompassed by Eurydice, who represents soul, conscience, maturity, muse and social identity, as well as lover, and the different outcomes in the three traditions, gave me a lot to play with. It gave me the opportunity to see Orpheus as many different artists – Seamus Heaney, Ted Hughes, Mick Jagger, Bob Dylan, Thomas the Rhymer and Gerald Way from the emo-band My Chemical Romance. I could use the multi-layered tradition to examine the use of poetry – and art in general; the role of an artist in society; the way an artist integrates – or fails to integrate – the practice of his art with his personal life, the nature of love, and the very odd relationship between artist and muse.

In my version, Eurydice is not dead or stolen by fairies; she is mad, and she and Orpheus are locked in a co-dependent relationship which may or may not destroy both of them. Whether either one of them gets out of hell depends on Orpheus' willingness to come to a sound understanding of who he is, and set Eurydice free to find her own salvation, on her own terms.

Orpheus Married

Sunlit Orpheus in the honeyed orchard
tuning the harp, trying out new lyrics,
watches her reading under the ympe tree.
She is his inspiration. She takes him
out beyond the utmost reach of humdrum
to nightmare palaces, cliffs of light.
He loves the bones of her, the angles where
another woman might have curves and softness,
bruise-dark eyes, blue veins under thin skin.
Her voice has rough edges. It shows the grain
where life has marked her. She is the key
to vision. What he has been looking for.

He domesticates her. Now she smiles sometimes,
puts on flesh. Her clothes are sometimes pretty.
He is devastated. Vigour from the root
has overwhelmed the grafted magic.
His Eurydice has become a stranger
This housewife in his bed is not his wife.

ympe tree: a grafted tree, distrusted because tampering with nature was thought to be impious if not actually dangerous. In medieval times sleeping under such a tree was believed to leave one vulnerable to the other-world, and the image of a grafted tree was sometimes used to symbolise a lack of integrity.

What the Harp Said

I am a high maintenance mistress.
You must carve me from your breast-bone,
string me with your love's golden hair,
give me unqualified devotion.

I will have the skin off your finger tips,
I will keep you from food, sleep, company.
I will let you tell secrets to me
and sing them on every street corner.

You must keep me safe as an egg
from the smallest signs of neglect.
I am demanding as peach blossom.
I don't perform in the cold.

I am a high maintenance mistress.
I leave nothing for anyone else.
But I sing like the wind in an ash tree,
like rain on a pool, like morning in autumn.

I speak unsought words of healing,
resolve confusion, stir dull feet to dance.
My strings hold voices that move the earth
and all of heaven's love-lit whirling spheres.

Breaking through Gravel

for Deborah

My Muses have nine children.
They go mad, lose their jobs,
live on rolled oats and vegetables.
That's how they write. In three languages,
in trains, in kitchens, in libraries,
on the back seat of the bus. They write
about sex and history and fairy tales,
the shape of a sonnet, splitting the atom,
where the rent is coming from. Their lives
are made of food, and soap, and meetings with strangers,
the family china, the slammed door, a child's stamped foot,
the hurt silence, the stolen kiss,
the need to write.
The art of women is not a quest, like the whale,
but salvage from a storm of perplexity.
It is unlicensed, illicit, defiant,
and inevitable as starlight,
or the trajectory of the lily of the valley
disregarding gravel, and breaking the tarmac
with unapologetic, overwhelming joy.

Digging for Bait

Sjussamillabakka –
da notes o' joy.
Stakkamillabakka –
da notes o' noy.
Sjussamillabakka –
da god gabber reel,
dat meicht ha' made a sick hert hale.

Sjussamillabakka-
between the sea and the shore.
Stakkamillabakka –
between the rocks and the shore.
Sjussamillabakka
is where he got this poem,
on water-polished shingle, where the sea
drains bubbling
over ribbed and wrinkled sand
and popping bladderwrack.
He found it in a rock-pool, cold as shadow,
with gull's feathers floating in it,
and a thin blue sheen of petrol
hazed like a mussel shell.

Sjussamillabakka –
the place without landmarks.
Stakkamillabakka –
don't look back.
Sjussamillabakka –
never the same place twice.

Sjussamillabakka and *stakkamillabakka* are Shetland words meaning 'between
the sea and the shore' and 'between the rocks and the shore' . If you ask a Shetland
fisherman where he got his bait from, he might answer '*sjussamillabakka*' - or
'*stakkamillabakka*'

What the Roadie Said

Turn up the echo, pal,
she's in the mood tonight.
Let the music simmer -
it's rohypnol to her.
Boil it up to candy height,
melt her thighs like fondant .

That's how he got the girls,
the voice mainly, the harp
was an extra. He'd get
those cold suburban chicks
mad as wasps on windfalls,
sweet and silly and hot.

After Eurydice
all that stopped. He never
looked sideways at a girl
until she left and then
it wasn't girls he wanted –
it was that other place.

He'd lost the appetite
for human company,
love's sweet salt common taste.
Mortal couldn't hold him,
he was outside, longing,
going somewhere else.

Turn up the Echo, or
was that some other girl?
another woman who
couldn't stand the way he
looked over his shoulder,
still wanting something more?

What Eurydice Said

Something about him, all wives say that -
pale-faced girls with black eyes,
scars where it doesn't show, or
hearts sucked dry as bank accounts -
there was something about the guy.

There was something about Orpheus
I think it was the way he had
of opening your mind's door to let
the wind blow in, with the tang of salt,
and rain-geese calling on the loch.

It didn't matter when he forgot
to come for meals, my birthday,
bills to pay. I didn't mind it
when he disappeared for days -
I never smelled a strange girl on him.

I loved him, that was all it was,
but still, I got to wanting
simple things, the ones I couldn't have -
fresh paint, trivial conversations,
tulips on the table, hope of children.

He didn't notice when I left,
not that I went anywhere at all.
I just got further in and deeper down
where silence was easier than tears,
and dark became seductive.

I let the cold king bring me here
across the knee-high bloody river,
and I wore my gown of fairies' green
among the ones who pay their tithe to hell
the ones men think are dead, and are not.

Sometimes I think of stars,
the flight of pigeons, and the way
a broom moves across a kitchen floor.
They belong to another country.
I have lost the tongue they speak there.

Moniage 1: Orpheus in the Wilderness

Orpheus deserts his post. Her flight
is like a magpie raid on his whole life -
what isn't gone is broken, pulled apart.
Only the harp goes with him, and he plays
in doorways, under arches, in the space
between the human places. When he sings,
the trees bend down to listen. No-one else will.

He is lost without her, and demented,
follows strange girls home, asks who's hiding her,
shouts obscenities at those who pass him by.
He hears voices in the dark, and follows them
out into wilder places, to be alone.

He comes on children, picking brambles,
noisy, carefree, quick and neat as birds.
They do not notice him, and go their way
unfrightened, and he hears the women call
them home to breakfast. When they are gone
the silence stirs him like a changing wind.
He says, "I used to do that, long ago."

He thinks of berries shining, intact, black,
the small hairs tickling his outstretched palm,
the scratches worn like war wounds, and the brag
of secret places, where there's loads still left.
That's when the door opens, the shadowed way
beneath the grey rock, to the other place.

The best known occurrence of moniage – in medieval English literature, a ritual time
of trial in the wilderness - is the obscure but charming poem Maiden on the Mor
Lay,which is referenced in Moniage 2.

Moniage 2: Orpheus Comes to the Gates of the Underworld

I on the moor lay, seven nights, seven years,
Until the earth's thin blood ran in my veins
Like peaty water running off the hill.
I fought the bee for honey, stole fish
From otters, drove the eagles from the hare.
I listened there to everything that moved,
Skylark, raven, and the dry sharp scrape
Of stone on stone. I heard the dead of winter,
And where the curlew poked his muddy bill,
I heard lost Eurydice call my name.

What was I looking for? I hardly knew –
A music speaking more to soul than heart,
Since hearts had failed me. I came at last
To a sea-cliff in the west, a warren
Full of wailing ghosts, shearwaters,
Gannets, petrels, kittiwake –
Lunatic, like the voices in my head.
A gull cried kee-yah! in the windy dark.
Morning, like an egg-shell cracked, and spilt
Warm bloody light upon the king's grey rock.

Orpheus in the Underworld

It's like two places. Look with one eye,
there's gold and feasting, girls in green velvet,
and music, light and joy. But look again.
Thin starved changelings, pale children in grey rags,
twittering like grasshoppers, unclaimed souls
not fit for hell or heaven, beautiful
and aimless, dangerous. This is the land
of eternal spring-time, which bears no fruit.

He sees Eurydice in a double vision,
a queen in cloth of gold, and a weeping girl
who cannot speak to him, who stretches out
cold arms, but slips away like air, like ghosts.
Which is truth, which is the phantom, who
is Eurydice, whom he says he loves?

Orpheus Plays 1: Callander Poetry Festival 2006

For Iyad Alhaiatly, a Palestinian poet, finally granted political asylum in December 2006

Poetry in the Garden starts
when Colin strikes the small Tibetan bowl.
The warmed and singing bronze awakes
A humming clarity, which sounds
through noise of knife and fork, book sales,
poets checking one another out,
and gathers stillness from the rainy night.
Later, Gaelic, Arabic and Greek
will take the song from tongue to tongue
goltraighe, geantraighe, suantraighe. It seems
presumptuous to claim
that poetry has power to move
much in the grinding moneyed world,
but Ayad, remember Orpheus
playing before the Faerie King,
on bagpipes, lyre or Breton harp,
the notes of sorrow, notes of joy and notes
of peace, while Hell falls silent.
All the cruel and unusual pain
stops for one moment, the lifeless courts
and derelict halls resounding
with the music, with the chance
for respite, wisdom, hope.

In classical Ireland proficiency in three modes of music was expected of a bard : Goltraighe, 'the weeping strain', here called 'da notes o' noy'; or lament, Geantriaghe, 'the laughing strain', here called 'da notes o' joy', or dance music; and Suantraighe, and 'the sleeping strain' or lullaby, which the ballad describes as 'da god gabber reel/dat meicht ha made a sick hert hale'. In Irish tradition the suantraighe makes anyone who is awake fall asleep, and anyone who is sick regain their health.

Orpheus Plays 2: Battlechant of the MCRmy

He has never seen the venue from this side.
Behind the amps, behind the rocksteady
cordon in liveried t-shirts, he has not seen
the broken vinyl, the congealed sweat
that drips like greasy rain, advertisements
for help-lines for the drugged, abused or disappeared.

From his side, in the stagelight bubble's
liquid pulsing, he sees glitterflashes,
a snowfall of shredded tickets, and the hands
waving when he waves, love graffiti
in tattoos and eyeliner, skull mittens,
fingers making horns. He hears the screaming,
singing in the pauses, maenad chanting
MCRmy! What is your profession?

He says he thinks of them as family.
They tell him how his music saved their lives.
He gives them songs of alienation
disillusionment, despair, death, pain and hell.
They sing too. They already know those words.
He tells them to be gentle to each other.
He comes downstage, takes the mike and shouts
I want to hear you mother-fuckers scream!

The MCRmy is the 'street team' of the rock band My Chemical Romance.
"What is your profession?" is the first half of the password on their web-site.

Orpheus Disputes with the Elf-King

Whoever made you, poet,
they did a wretched job of it.
There are holes in your brain I see stars through
and your words are broken like your shoes.
You smell of smoke and magic.
How can you be trusted with love?

I am a poet
I cannot be trusted with cliché,
with icons or prejudice or half-truth.
A poet is no more and no less to be trusted
than anyone else, but this I know.
Poets belong to their people
and love is the whole of our craft.

How far do you have to be
up yourself to be a poet?
How far does your - shall we call it – art
justify this kind of behaviour?
Tell me why you're here,
and while you're at it, tell me,
just who do you think you are?

I am a poet.
I sing at the feasts of kings
I welcome the new-born with lullabies
and put the bride to bed
with sweet epithalamions.

You are a poet.
You sell your verses for money,
for reviews and residencies.
You celebrate the opening of lottery purses
the flowing champagne and the fat slapped backs
of men in grey suits.

I am a poet.
I am learned in genealogies.
I know where the warriors fell in battle –
who died well, and who lies face down in the bog
with the broad of a sword in his back.
I can raise spots of three colours
on the face of the fairest.
Statesmen and false prophets have died of my venom.

You are a poet.
You betrayed three women who loved you.
Your debts are unpaid and your children
go shoeless, or live in other men's houses.
You do not even appear to have wit
enough to come in from the cold.

I am a poet.
I have heard the ceol n-a mara
in the white streams on the hill-side.
I have heard the strange song
of the baleen whale in the depths of the sea.
I have learned to walk in humility.
I have learned to speak of peace.

Those are big and easy words, poet,
and you will have no use for them.
Once you return to daylight with your wife
your life will be paper, milk and blood,
soap in the eyes, skelfs in the finger,
ashes, wet feet, the taste of apples.
You will make your poems with that.

I will be a poet.
And all the words will be available to me.
My wife will sing to my children
in the garden we will make together,
and welcome neighbours will listen to songs
of work and weather, the flight of birds,
the way the sun dreams in the deep pools.
I have not done with vision. It belongs to them.

The *ceol n-a mara* (lit. 'song of the sea') is supposed to be the music of
the other-world, the 'greyworld', when heard in mortal lands - the 'greenworld'.

The Judgement of Persephone

Orpheus is always coming here.
He hangs about the hills and hollow tracks
in various incarnations, and each one
looking, he says, for something he has lost,
a haunting he can neither name nor catch.

I don't deny that he can play a bit.
The Clashing Rocks stood still to hear him once
and sirens died for envy of his voice-
they're round the palace somewhere, sulking yet.
It's just I'm not impressed. I hate the way
He tries to use his talent like a bribe,
The cocky stance, that cute spontaneous smile
That says he knows I can't resist him.

Sometimes he's hooked on eerie, glamoured by
the whole dysfunction zoo. He feeds on it.
No love of his gets out of here alive.
He doesn't always make it out himself.
I've been there. When I came here and ate
those pomegranate seeds I thought I'd found
the truth my mother hid from me. I didn't know
you can't be dead unless you've been alive.

Sometimes it's different, you can see it -
When the music plays, it's her he plays for,
Now it's her I watch. His Eurydice,
Herodys, his queen, the lady Isobel.
She watches him, and then I get it.
Not self-sufficient then, not posturing,
not shaman, but a man who sings to share
his vision, one who knows his need for love.

That poet is the one whose plea I hear.

What the Maenad Said

When Orpheus came home,
in his torn coat and broken sandals,
his matted dreadlocks smelled of woodsmoke
and his face was grey with rain and mud.

When Orpheus came home,
he was over-ready to answer questions.
He said 'Aye, aye, I've seen that country.'
He had forgotten her name.

When Orpheus came home,
he would no longer play for weddings.
He accosted strangers in the street.
Dogs barked at him as he passed.

When Orpheus came home
Three of his harp-strings were broken.
He played like the wind in a cracked chimney.
He sang like a seal on a rock.

Eurydice Rising

For Naomi

Now Orpheus lays a still hand on the harp
and music ceases. He walks unfaltering
through the honest gates of horn
to reclaim earth-light, the music of the folk,
the feel of dirt beneath his fingers.

Eurydice hears him. It is like
the ends of songs in Ireland,
which the singer speaks, not sings,
to break the spell. She awakes from dreams
and discovers starry twilight.

She follows him through wells of light
and morning's ticker-tape parades
of skylark song and rain.
He does not know new colours
bloom in her cheeks and eyes.
He does not see her dancing.

He sees the daylight hang out banners
above the homely fields and town
and blesses every sleeping soul within.
And then, the fairytale conclusion -
he finds beyond his garden gate,
in the orchard, sunlit Eurydice.